The OJIBWE

People, Culture, and History

by Kim Sigafus

T0400521

CAPSTONE PRESS
a capstone imprint

Published by Capstone Press, an imprint of Capstone
1710 Roe Crest Drive, North Mankato, Minnesota 56003
capstonepub.com

Library of Congress Cataloging-in-Publication Data is available on the Library of Congress website.

ISBN: 9798875208584 (hardcover)
ISBN: 9798875208539 (paperback)
ISBN: 9798875208546 (ebook PDF)

Summary: The traditions, culture, and history of the Ojibwe people are told through engaging text, sidebars, activities, maps, and more.

Editorial Credits
Editor: Erika L. Shores; Designer: Heidi Thompson; Media Researcher: Rebekah Hubstenberger; Production Specialist: Tori Abraham

Image Credits
Alamy: Carlos Gonzalez/Minneapolis Star Tribune/ZUMA Press Inc, 28, Eric Engman/Fairbanks Daily News-Miner/ZUMAPRESS.com, 22, Jeffrey Isaac Greenberg 17+, 21, North Wind Picture Archives, 11, Science History Images, 8; Associated Press: Aaron Lavinsky/Star Tribune, 16, Ellen Schmidt/The Minnesota Daily, 24, Jessie Wardarski, 13; Getty Images: Bettmann, 14, Richard Tsong-Taatarii/Star Tribune, 29, Tim M Lanthier, 19, Werner Forman/Universal Images Group, 26; Newscom: Angel Wynn / DanitaDelimont.com / "Danita Delimont Photography," 7, cover; Shutterstock: Bardocz Peter, 4, Jamey Penney-Ritter, 20, MaraZe, 23 (textured paper), Pyty, 5, Qamza, 18, Runrun2 (brush stroke), cover, spine, 1, Svetlana Zhukova, 17

Printed and bound in the USA. 006307

TABLE OF CONTENTS

Words in **bold** are in the glossary.

ABOUT THE OJIBWE

Who Are the Ojibwe?

The Ojibwe, also known as the Chippewa, are an Algonquin-speaking tribe who primarily live in Minnesota, Michigan, North Dakota, Wisconsin, and Ontario, Manitoba, and Saskatchewan, Canada. They are known as the Anishinaabe or First People. Originally from the East, they eventually settled in these areas in the mid-1700s.

Who Are the Algonquians?

The Algonquians are a group of tribes who traditionally spoke similar languages and lived in the same ways. They are made up of many tribes, including the Ojibwe, Shawnee, and Cree.

Ojibwe Reservations and Reserves

The Ojibwe are the largest **Indigenous** group in North America. Federal reservations are in Minnesota, Michigan, Wisconsin, Montana, and North Dakota. In Canada, Ojibwe reserves are located in Ontario, Manitoba, and Saskatchewan.

What Are Reservations?

Two hundred years ago through a series of broken **treaties**, or agreements, with the governments of Canada or the United States, the Indigenous people of North America lost most of their land. They were put on reservations or reserves, which were lands the government gave them to live on. Today there are approximately 326 reservations in the U.S., and in Canada there are 3,394 reserves.

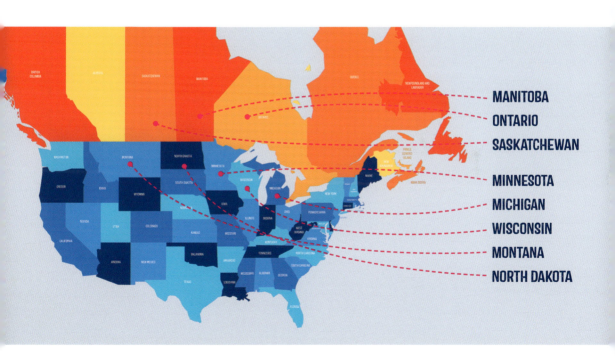

MANITOBA

ONTARIO

SASKATCHEWAN

MINNESOTA

MICHIGAN

WISCONSIN

MONTANA

NORTH DAKOTA

AN OJIBWE CELEBRATION

The smells of fry bread surround you. You can feel the beat of the big drum in your chest. It is the steady heartbeat of mother earth. The colorful **regalia**, the singing and dancing, all tell you that you are at a powwow.

For centuries, Indigenous people have held ceremonial gatherings. The powwow is an important celebration in Ojibwe **culture**. It gives them a chance to share their traditions with non-Native people through food, dance, music, and crafts. It is also a time to sing and dance together, renew old friendships, and make new ones. The modern-day powwow most people are familiar with started in the early 1800s.

A young dancer performs at a powwow on the Rocky Boy Indian Reservation in Montana.

OJIBWE HISTORY

In the tradition story, the Anishinaabe, or Ojibwe, were living on the east coast near the Gulf of St. Lawrence in Canada 1,500 years ago. The Great Prophesy came to be from their medicine man. He had a vision that big boats would be traveling across the water to their land. These boats would bring with them disease. The Ojibwe made the decision to move. The megis (turtle) shell would guide their travels. They would know when to stop when they found the food that grows on water. This food would later be known as wild rice.

It took hundreds of years for the Ojibwe people to migrate to Michigan, and later Wisconsin on Madeline Island in Chequamegon Bay, Lake Superior. Eventually they spread out, moving inland in 1745, and settling in Minnesota around the same time. This is where they found wild rice.

The Ojibwe built dome-shaped homes called wigwams.

Timeline

1500 The Anishinaabe, or Ojibwe, settle in the Great Lakes region, near Makinak Minissing and the Great Falls.

1615 French explorer Samuel de Champlain arrives at Lake Huron, where some Ojibwe live.

1693 Madeline Island becomes the center of the Ojibwe Nation.

1745 Chief Keeshkemun settles his band of Ojibwe in the area now known as Lac du Flambeau in Wisconsin.

1825 Treaty of Prairie du Chien establishes border between Dakota and Ojibwe in the territory of Michigan.

1830 Indian Removal Act passed.

1837 The Ojibwe sign the Treaty of St. Peters, selling most of their land in north-central Wisconsin and eastern Minnesota to the U.S. government.

1854 The Ojibwe sign the Treaty of La Pointe, ceding their homeland to the United States and establishing reservations for four Ojibwe bands in Wisconsin.

1913 The White Earth Roll Commission hires anthropologists to determine who is Ojibwe by blood.

1934 Indian Reorganization Act is passed. Its goal is to secure new rights for Native Americans on reservations.

1969 National Indian Education Association is founded to give American Indians, Alaska Natives, and Native Hawaiians a national voice in education.

1983 Ojibwe in Wisconsin reclaim treaty rights to hunt and fish on land they ceded in 1837 and 1842.

2021 Ojibwe author Louise Erdrich wins a Pulitzer Prize for her book *The Night Watchman*.

In the late 1700s and early 1800s, **colonizers** spread westward into the areas where the Ojibwe lived. In 1830, the Indian Removal Act passed. This meant Native people were to be removed from their lands and sent west of the Mississippi River. It took until 1850 for the removal process to reach northern Wisconsin.

Over the years, the Ojibwe signed treaties that gave their homelands to the U.S. government. In exchange, the government was supposed to make payments of money and supplies to the Ojibwe. These payments were called annuities.

U.S. President Zachary Taylor eventually signed an order to move Lake Superior Ojibwe from Wisconsin to Minnesota. To force them to relocate, they told them they would have to go to Sandy Lake in central Minnesota to pick up their annuities. It was hoped they would go to Minnesota and not return to Wisconsin.

Chief Keckewaishke

Even as a young warrior, Kechewaishke was known to use peaceful tactics when dealing with the U.S. government. He was born in 1759. Due to his abilities in hunting and battle, he was recognized as an Ojibwe chief and primary spokesman for all the bands. He was a key figure in stopping the Indian removal after the Sandy Lake Tragedy that led to hundreds of deaths in 1850.

In October 1850, the Ojibwe traveled to Sandy Lake. When they arrived, there was no money or supplies. They waited for weeks, starving and freezing, and many of them became sick and died. Many died on the way home from there. These events are now known as the Sandy Lake Tragedy.

Around 5,000 Ojibwe traveled to Sandy Lake. Around 400 died at the lake or on their way back home.

Daily life is now different for the Ojibwe. While some people remain on the reservations set up for them by the government, many people live and work in bigger cities. Whether they stay on reservation land or not, the Ojibwe hold on to their culture and incorporate it into their lives.

It's been a hard road for Ojibwe to carry on their culture and traditions. Many Ojibwe Elders were sent to **boarding schools** when they were young. In the 1800s and 1900s, hundreds of thousands of Indigenous children in the United States and Canada were removed from their families and cultures.

The U.S. and Canadian governments wanted to separate Indigenous children from their culture and traditions. The governments wanted to end their spiritual practices and languages. They would be replaced with European customs and language.

A Leech Lake Band of Ojibwe Elder sprinkles tobacco into the water. This tradition is to give thanks before harvesting wild rice from the lake.

At boarding schools, Ojibwe children were punished for speaking their languages and practicing their culture. Minnesota had 16 boarding schools and Wisconsin had 11. By 1970 most of them had closed. The Ojibwe are now working hard to bring back their language and traditions, so they won't be lost for future generations.

Through education, the Ojibwe connect and preserve their culture. In 1969, the National Indian Education Association (NIEA) was founded in Minneapolis. It gives American Indians, Alaska Natives, and Native Hawaiians a voice in education. The NIEA supports continuous use of Indigenous languages and traditional knowledge in schools and educational centers.

Dennis Banks

Dennis Banks was a teacher, author, and activist. He was born on Leech Lake Indian Reservation in Minnesota in 1937. At age 5, he was taken and sent to a boarding school. As he grew up, he knew he had to change the way his people were being treated. In 1968, he cofounded the American Indian Movement in Minneapolis with Vernon Bellecourt. The organization works on issues of poverty, police brutality, and discrimination.

The Ojibwe Language

People work to preserve the Ojibwe language. Language classes are taught at schools and colleges on reservations. You can practice writing and saying these Ojibwe words.

boozhoo (boo-zoo)—hello

daga (daa-gaa)—please

eya' (aya)—yes

gaawiin (gaa-ween)—no

gigawaabamin menawaa (gig-a-waa-baa-min mee-naa-waa)—There is no word for "goodbye" in the Ojibwe language. This phrase means, "So long until I see you again."

imbaabaa (im-baa-baa)—my father

miigwech (mee-gwich)—thank you

nimaamaa (ni-maa-maa)—my mother

nimishoomis (nim-i-shoo-mis)—my grandfather

nookomis (nook-oh-mis)—my grandmother

OJIBWE CULTURE

Hunting, fishing, and planting and harvesting food has always been a part of Ojibwe culture. Today, many Ojibwe plant gardens. The Three Sisters planting has been done for hundreds of years. Beans, corn, and squash are known as the Three Sisters. This way of planting is also called "companion planting."

As Native people plant their gardens now, they try to work in the same traditional ways. Corn is planted first, and then the beans. The beans use the cornstalk to climb up and grow on. Squash is planted last around the base of the planting. This chokes out weeds and put nutrients into the soil. Growing the three plants together in this way results in a better harvest.

Winona LaDuke

Winona LaDuke is an activist who works to help Indigenous populations across the United States. She ran for U.S. vice president with Ralph Nader in 1996 and 2000. She has co-authored many books including *All Our Relations: Native Struggles for Land and Life*. Today, LaDuke devotes much of her time to farming on the White Earth Reservation in Minnesota, where she grows heritage vegetables and hemp.

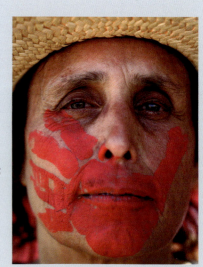

The Three Sisters planting is corn, squash, and beans.

FRY BREAD

Fry bread was a necessary food in the Ojibwe people's lives for a long time. After the U.S. government decided to move all the Ojibwe people onto reservation land, they also promised them annuities that included food. Ojibwe were given flour, beef, beans, bacon, sugar, lard, coffee, and tobacco. Often, these foods were full of bugs and stale.

The Ojibwe people made the best of what they had. In adding some of the ingredients together, fry bread was created. Although it is a simple food, for Native people it represents resilience and strength. It is still made for family meals and events. Its recipe has been expanded to include many toppings including taco seasonings. It can be made with a hole in the middle for less puffiness.

Fry bread is made from flour, baking powder, salt, and water. It is then fried in oil or lard.

Many people add taco toppings to fry bread.

THE JINGLE DRESS

In 1918, the Jingle Dress came to the Ojibwe in a dream of an Ojibwe man whose daughter was ill. In the dream, he was told to make the dress and have her dance in it. If he did this, she would be healed.

The man and his wife quickly set about making the dress and helped their daughter into it. After several days of dancing, she was healed.

This traditional story quickly spread to other Native tribes. They have adopted the story and the dress. It is known as a healing dress. Traditionally made with 365 jingles, the jingles were rolled up can lids that would make a sound when sewn next to each other on the dress. People still make and wear the dress today for all types of events.

BASKET MAKING

The Ojibwe are known for making birchbark and sweetgrass baskets. Mothers passed the skills on to their daughters. One technique used to make Ojibwe sweetgrass baskets is coiling, which involves sewing plant fibers around a foundation material in spirals, with each spiral sewn to the one before it.

Baskets were used to hold and carry things in. Birchbark baskets have been used for hundreds of years to harvest wild rice. Modern baskets are also made for gifts. Many museums display these beautiful baskets, having been donated by modern basket makers and Native tribes.

Recipe with Wild Rice

Ojibwe baskets were used to hold the wild rice harvest. Wild rice was a main food for the Ojibwe. This soup includes wild rice and is the author's family recipe. Ask an adult to help you.

Ingredients

- 1 package (6.2-ounce) quick-cooking long grain and wild rice mix
- ¼ teaspoon ground black pepper
- 3½ cups chicken stock
- 2 tablespoons butter
- 1½ cups shiitake mushrooms, cut the stems off and then cut up
- 1 cup celery stalks, cut up
- 2 cups chopped cooked turkey
- 1 cup whipping cream

Instructions

1. Prepare the rice mix according to package directions, except don't use any butter. Set it aside.

2. Using a big saucepan, melt butter, then add the pepper, celery, and mushrooms.

3. Cook it stirring once in a while for about 8 minutes until tender and the liquid is almost gone.

4. Add chicken stock. Bring to a boil and then reduce the heat.

5. Cover the pan and simmer for about 7 minutes.

6. Stir in cooked rice mixture, turkey, and whipping cream.

7. Cook it all together and serve.

OJIBWE DRUMS

As with every culture, music is a huge part of life. Drums are an important part of Ojibwe culture. There are several types of Native drums with specific functions depending on the ceremony. These include the water drums for special ceremonies. Hand drums can be used for day-to-day activities like quietly singing a baby to sleep. The powwow drums are mighty and fierce, and traditionally only men play them while they sing.

Drums are considered living objects that can be passed down from one generation to the next. Typically, there is a drum keeper. This person takes responsibility for the care of the drums.

Talking Feather Craft

A talking feather is used by the Ojibwe during storytelling. The person holding the talking feather has everyone's attention while speaking. You can make your own talking feather.

What You Need

- feather, at least 6 inches long

- artificial sinew (found at craft stores)

- fabric glue

- leather lacing

- beads

What You Do

1. Hold the feather upright in one hand and start wrapping the sinew down the quill of the feather. Make sure the sinew covers most of the quill but leave some space at the bottom otherwise it will all come off.

2. Glue the end of the sinew down with fabric glue.

3. Cut two 5-inch pieces of sinew and tie each in a knot around the top of the quill.

4. Slide the number of beads you want onto the two pieces of sinew hanging down.

5. When done, either make a knot on each string, or tie the last bead onto the string.

6. Cut an 8-inch piece of leather lacing and tie it in a bow on the top of the quill.

7. Hang your feather on the wall or lay it in a special place.

WRITING HISTORY

The Ojibwe have a history that was written on rock walls and birchbark scrolls. This helped keep their history alive. Their writings were able to be passed down from one generation to the next. The scrolls included their migration story and use symbols and patterns.

Many Native authors continue passing on stories through their books. Louise Erdrich is an Ojibwe author from Minnesota who writes poetry, novels, and children's books. Thomas D. Peacock is from the Fond du Lac Band of Lake Superior Anishinaabe Ojibwe. He wrote *The Good Path*. This children's book is filled with traditional tales.

An Ojibwe birchbark scroll

The Ojibwe Creation Story

In this story, the author retells the Ojibwe tale of how the world came to be.

Long, long ago, Gitchie Manidoo (Great Spirit) looked down from his place in the sky and saw his people struggling. They were addressing the world with unkindness. He decided to rid the world of these people and start over.

He sent a great flood. It wiped out everything except some flying birds and swimming animals. He also left one man, Nanaboozhoo (First Man) floating on a log in the middle of the water.

Nanaboozhoo had been on that log for weeks and was getting tired of floating there. He asked the animals swimming around him if they could dive down in the water to bring up some land from the bottom. They dove down but were unsuccessful.

Muskrat wanted to help. Nanaboozhoo watched Muskrat dive down into the water. Eventually, the lifeless body of Muskrat came floating up to the surface. Nanaboozhoo sadly picked up his friend and laid him on the log. As he did so, the body rolled over and Nanaboozhoo could see that in Muskrat's paw was dirt.

He carefully took the dirt. With a prayer to Gitchie Manidoo, he raised his hands and land came up from the bottom of the water. Nanaboozhoo paddled his log to the land and got off. With Gitchie Manidoo's help, he recreated everything in the world.

He hadn't forgotten Muskrat. He gathered the creatures and said, "This is our friend Muskrat, who gave his life so we could start over."

Then he saw a big turtle swimming by. He lay Muskrat's body down and gathered the world up into a ball and laid it on the turtle's back. He knew if a great flood came again, everyone would be all right, for the world was now floating on a turtle's back.

OJIBWE INVENTIONS

People everywhere use many items invented by the Ojibwe. Canoes were originally made from birchbark so Ojibwe people could fish and travel the waters near their homelands. The Ojibwe also created their own design for snowshoes that were used in the winter for walking through deep snow. Their version of the hammock is still used today too.

Snowshoes are attached to boots to help walk across snow.

Ojibwe use canoes to harvest wild rice.

The Ojibwe also contributed to the American way of life by discovering maple syrup and wild rice. Both foods are still harvested and included in family recipes.

Many cities and states have Ojibwe names. Mississippi is from the Ojibwe word, Misi-ziibi. It means "big river" referring to the longest river in North America. Mishigamaa means "great water," and is the Ojibwe word for the state of Michigan. Through words, inventions, music, food, and more, Ojibwe culture and history are kept alive and celebrated.

Glossary

boarding school (BOR-ding SKOOL)—a place where students live while they are going to school at the same time

colonizer (KAH-luh-nye-zur)—a nation or government that claims a territory other than its own

culture (KUHL-chur)—the traditions, beliefs, and behaviors that a group of people share

Indigenous (in-DIJ-eh-nus)—the first to live in a place

regalia (re-GALE-ee-uh)—special clothes that are worn for powwows or other special occasions

treaty (TREE-tee)—a written agreement between two groups

Read More

Peacock, Thomas. *The Forever Sky*. St. Paul, MN: Minnesota Historical Society Press, 2019.

Rendon, Marcie. *Stitches of Tradition (Gashkigwaaso Tradition)*. New York: Heartdrum, 2024.

Treuer, Anton. *Everything You Wanted to Know About Indians But Were Afraid to Ask*. Hoboken, NJ: Levine Querido, 2021.

Internet Sites

Mille Lacs Band of Ojibwe: Culture
millelacsband.com/home/culture

Red Rock Indian Band: Our Culture
rrib.ca/our-culture

St. Croix Chippewa Indians of Wisconsin: Who We Are
stcroixojibwe-nsn.gov/culture/who-we-are

Index

About the Author

An award-winning Ojibwe author and speaker, Kim Sigafus writes Native fiction and nonfiction. Her work includes The Mida series, about a mystically powerful time-traveling carnival; and a young adult series on bullying. Her nonfiction work includes *Native Elders*, and the award-winning *Native Writers*. She is an Illinois Humanities Road Scholar speaker. She travels the Midwest speaking on her culture. She lives in Freeport, Illinois, with her husband, Andy. Learn more about Kim at kimberlysigafus.com.